Also by James W. Gaynor
Everything Becomes a Poem

Jane Austen's
PRIDE AND PREJUDICE
in
61 Haiku
(1,037 Syllables!)

James W. Gaynor
(#HaikuJim)

facebook.com/NemetonPress
NemetonPress@gmail.com
240 East 76 Street, 15W, New York, NY 10021

ISBN 978-0-9978428-3-8 (paperback)
First Edition
Designed by: pak creative, pakcreative.com
Authur photo credit: Justin Wilson
Printed and bound by: IngramSpark

7 October 2020

for Paul

This book is dedicated to all
who read the first line of *Pride and Prejudice*
and felt as though the top of their heads
had been taken off.

Infinities of love

*(Austen's closing salutation
for the two or three
people she actually
liked)*

The Power of the Perfect Pick-Up Line — Jane Austen Makes Her Move

Emily Dickinson once famously remarked that if she felt as though the top of her head were taken off, she knew she was reading poetry. And who among us did not read "It is a truth universally acknowledged, ..." and feel our heads explode?

In what must be one of English literature's most quoted opening sentences, the narrator zeroes in on her reader and introduces herself with essentially the perfect pick-up line.

Austen continues to flirt with her reader in the first sentences of each of the book's 61 chapters. So, how better to acknowledge the power of her collective one-line poetry than by translating *Pride and Prejudice's* opening-sentence poems into contemporary twists on the classic Japanese 17-syllable haiku? And here you have it: *Jane Austen's Pride and Prejudice in 61 Haiku (1,037 Syllables!).*

It is my hope that readers will find themselves smiling knowingly from time to time as they travel in this redesigned Japanese vehicle across Austen's familiar English landscape — and that they will forgive my star-struck attempt at this love-letter-poem to the extraordinary woman who still speaks to us in ways that can blast off the top of our heads.

— **JAMES W. GAYNOR**
(#HaikuJim)
jameswgaynor.com

Volume One

CHAPTER 1.

It is a truth universally acknowledged, that a single man in possession of a good fortune, must be in want of a wife.

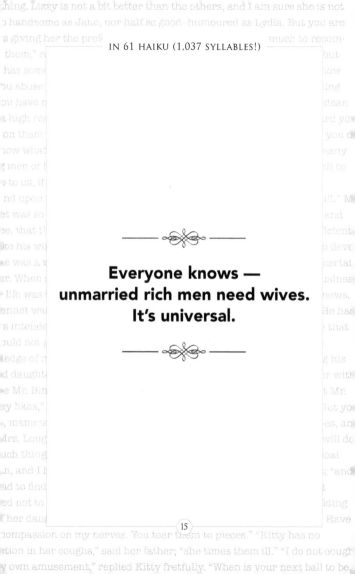

thing. Lizzy is not a bit better than the others; and I am sure she is not so handsome as Jane, nor half so good-humoured as Lydia. But you are always giving her the pref...   ...much to recommend them," re...   ...but has some...   ...how you abuse...   ...ing you have r...   ...dear. a high re...   ...rd you on them...   ...you d now what...   ...hany g men of f...   ...ill be e to us. if...   ...nd upon...   ...il." M et was so...   ...and ee, that th...   ...ficient ke his wi...   ...o deve e was a v...   ...certai er. When...   ...usines life was...   ...news. ennet wa...   ...He ha s intends...   ...e that ould not...   ...ledge of it...   ...g his d daughte...   ...r with e Mr. Bir...   ...t Mr. ey likes,"...   ...But yo e, mamma...   ...es, an Mrs. Long...   ...will do uch thing...   ...ical n, and I h...   ...; "and ad to find...   ...ed not to...   ...lding her daug...   ...Have

**Everyone knows —
unmarried rich men need wives.
It's universal.**

compassion on my nerves. You tear them to pieces." "Kitty has no ...tion in her coughs," said her father; "she times them ill." "I do not cough ...y own amusement," replied Kitty fretfully. "When is your next ball to be,

CHAPTER 2.

Mr. Bennet was among the earliest of those who waited on Mr. Bingley.

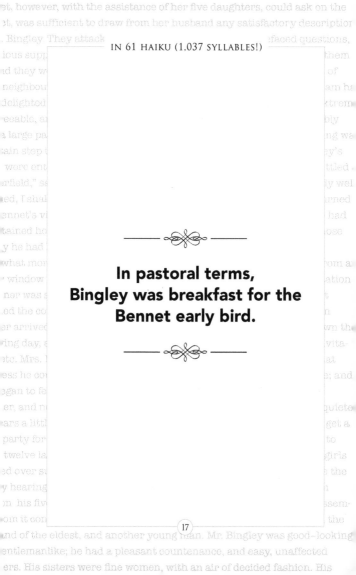

In pastoral terms,
Bingley was breakfast for the
Bennet early bird.

CHAPTER 3.

Not all that Mrs. Bennet, however, with the assistance of her five daughters, could ask on the subject, was sufficient to draw from her husband any satisfactory description of Mr. Bingley.

are say very agreeable. Do let me ask my partner to introduce you."

do you mean?" and turning round he looked for a moment at Elizabeth

ching her eye, he wi...   he is tolerable,

No one could find out
if Charles Bingley was handsome.
Not that it mattered.

the two next. Then the two third he danced with Miss King, and the

rth with Maria Lucas, and the two fifth with Jane again, and the two

with Lizzy, and the Boulanger." "If he had had any compassion for me,"

CHAPTER 4.

When Jane and Elizabeth were alone, the former, who had been cautious in her praise of Mr. Bingley before, expressed to her sister just how very much she admired him.

**Jane told Lizzy she
admired Mr. Bingley.
And so it began.**

CHAPTER 5.

Within a short walk of Longbourn lived a family with whom the Bennets were particularly intimate.

Jane, I suppose, because he danced with her twice. To be sure that did
as if he admired her indeed I rather believe he did I heard something
it but I hardly know   son." "Perhaps yo
what I ev   n it to
Mr Robin   nd
her he did   room,
hich he tl   he las
on: "Oh! t   wo
ons on tha   d th
seem as if
earrings v   "M
r is not so   b be
ust tolera   xed b
-treatme   e a
rtune to l   lose to
r half-an
n? is not   rey
ing to her   rfield
e could n   y at
spoke to.   s muc
s among l
able." "I d
able, he w
body says
now that l   ball in
chaise." "   as, "b
. he had d   . "I
. not dano
se you ne   s not
l me so m   One
t wonder   ythin
favour, si   s a
to be pro   aily

IN 61 HAIKU (1,037 SYLLABLES!)

**Life in the country
was tedious. Neighbors helped
relieve the boredom.**

23

e his pride, if he had not mortified mine." "Pride," observed Mary, who
d herself upon the solidity of her reflections, "is a very common failing, I
e By all that I have ever read, I am convinced that it is very common

CHAPTER 6.

The ladies of Longbourn soon waited on those of Netherfield.

do more than like her, if she does not help him on." "But she does help

, as much as her nature will allow. If I can perceive her regard for him,

st be a simpleton, in

ember, Eliza,

does no

to a mai   t."

ps he nu   e

olerably   ways

h other   t

be empl   the

f every   she

re of hin   she

s." "You   in

on but th   o get

usband.   re

he's facli   be

of the d   is

him onl   on;

w him on   n in

ny four t   is

ter." "No   e

only hav   st

ber that

gs may   em

rtain th   h

t to any   has

nfolded."   eart;

she were   d a

of happ   ive-

Happin   si-

f the par   ar

hand, it

e to gro

on; and

———— ❦ ————

Visits were exchanged.
The women all cordially
hated each other.

———— ❦ ————

with whom you are to pass your life." "You make me laugh, Charlotte;
s not sound. You know it is not sound, and that you would never act in
y yourself." Occupied in observing Mr. Bingley's attentions to her

25

CHAPTER 7.

Mr. Bennet's property consisted almost entirely in an estate of two thousand a year, which, unfortunately for his daughters, was entailed, in default of heirs male, on a distant relation; and their mother's fortune, though ample for her situation in life, could but ill supply the deficiency of his.

— ❧ —

**Five Bennet daughters —
estate planning gone awry.
Which explains a lot.**

— ❧ —

§ CHAPTER 8.

At five o'clock the two ladies retired to dress, and at half-past six Elizabeth was summoned to dinner.

married to a Mr. Phillips, who had been a clerk to their father and
eded him in the business, and a brother settled in London in a respect-
ine of trade. The vula   e from Meryton; a
convenie   ed
er three o   a
er's shop   ring
ydia, wer   ore
vacant th   k to
ton was n   ersa-
or the eve   ight
ey alway: ced,
were well   rival c
tia regim   ter,
Meryton w   ow

active of t   ng to
knowledg   were
ng a secr   ves.
hillips vis   ity
own befor   y's
fortune, t

The Bingley sisters required ninety minutes to gild their lilies.

less in th   fter
ing one r   ly
ved: "Fro   st be
f the sillie   I am
onvinced   Lydia
perfect in   in
r, and ha   ng th
morning   "that
hould be   ink
ingly of a   "If my
en are si
ens, they   er
f, on whi   ided

particular, but I must so far differ from you as to think our two younger
aters uncommonly foolish." "My dear Mr. Bennet, you must not expect
girls to have the sense of their father and mother. When they get to our

CHAPTER 9.

Elizabeth passed the chief of the night in her sister's room, and in the morning had the pleasure of being able to send a tolerable answer to the inquiries which she very early received from Mr. Bingley by a housemaid, and some time afterwards from the two elegant ladies who waited on his sisters.

**Everyone hoped —
for different reasons — Jane
was feeling better.**

10

CHAPTER 10.

The day passed much as the day before had done.

How time flies when one's having fun! Which was not the case at Netherfield.

wish with all my heart she were well settled. But with such a father and
r, and such low connections, I am afraid there is no chance of it." "I thin
heard you say that their uncle is an attorney on Meryton." "Yes; and

CHAPTER 11.

When the ladies removed after dinner, Elizabeth ran up to her sister, and seeing her well guarded from cold, attended her into the drawing-room, where she was welcomed by her two friends with many professions of pleasure; and Elizabeth had never seen them so agreeable as they were during the hour which passed before the gentlemen appeared.

ilities, Charles." "Upon my word, Caroline. I should think it more
le to get Pemberley by purchase than by imitation." Elizabeth was so
caught with what pa   ention for her
and soon

ned hers   e
"Is Miss   "will
as tall as   l
t's height   et
nybody w   nners
o extreme   ne-
s exquisi   ean
patience t   les
plished!   think
all paint t   one
annot do   of for
st time. w   "Your
the comr   ah

The word   se
y nettin   eeing
ou in you   g
than half   e
accompl   rved
eth, "yo   lished
n." "Yes,   his
l assista   s not
y surpass   h
edge of r   es, to
ve the wo   hing
r and ma   pres-
or the wo

Darcy, "   al, in
provema   rprise
r knowir   your

IN 61 HAIKU (1,037 SYLLABLES!)

The Bingley sisters
were almost bearable when
the men were absent.

35

ng any." "Are you so severe upon your own sex as to doubt the possibilit
his?" "I never saw such a woman. I never saw such capacity, and taste,
plication, and elegance, as you describe united." Mrs. Hurst and Miss

otesting that they knew many women who answered this description, w
. Hurst called them to order, with bitter complaints of their inattention
at was going f   by at an end, Elizab

CHAPTER 12.

In consequence of an agreement
between the sisters, Elizabeth
wrote the next morning to their
mother, to beg that the carriage
might be sent for them in the
course of the day.

r recovering immediately, as her restoration to health would probably
move her from Netherfield. She would not listen, therefore, to her daught
posal of being carried home; neither did the apothecary who arrived

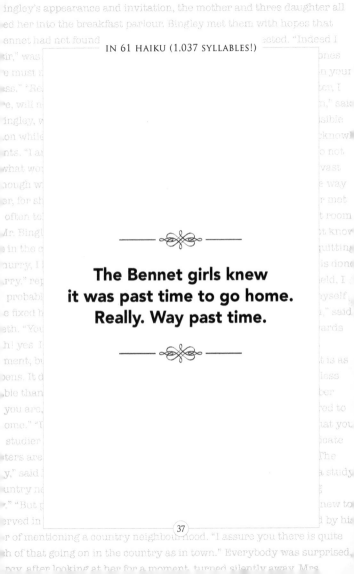

ingley's appearance and invitation, the mother and three daughter all
ed her into the breakfast parlour. Bingley met them with hopes that
ennet had not found ... ected. "Indeed I

IN 61 HAIKU (1,037 SYLLABLES!)

The Bennet girls knew
it was past time to go home.
Really. Way past time.

r of mentioning a country neighbourhood. "I assure you there is quite
h of that going on in the country as in town." Everybody was surprised,
nev after looking at her for a moment, turned silently away. Mrs

CHAPTER 13.

"I hope, my dear," said Mr. Bennet to his wife, as they were at breakfast the next morning, "that you have ordered a good dinner to-day, because I have reason to expect an addition to our family party."

en many a one, I fancy, overcome in the same way. I wonder who first ⟨discov⟩ered the efficacy of poetry in driving away love!" "I have been used to ⟨consider⟩ poetry as the food

There was no good way to break the news about this houseguest's arrival.

ot." Mrs. Bennet and her daughters then departed, and Elizabeth ⟨return⟩ed instantly to Jane, leaving her own and her relations' behaviour to the ⟨remar⟩ks of the two ladies and Mr. Darcy; the latter of whom, however, could

CHAPTER 14.

During dinner, Mr. Bennet scarcely spoke at all; but when the servants were withdrawn, he thought it time to have some conversation with his guest, and therefore started a subject in which he expected him to shine, by observing that he seemed very fortunate in his patroness.

CHAPTER 15.

Mr. Collins was not a sensible man, and the deficiency of nature had been but little assisted by education or society; the greatest part of his life having been spent under the guidance of an illiterate and miserly father; and though he belonged to one of the universities, he had merely kept the necessary terms, without forming at it any useful acquaintance.

e he disliked her, was still more strange. She could only imagine,

r, at last that she drew his notice because there was something more

and reprehensible, s   n in any other per

esent. Th   care

approba   d the

by a live   ar

th, said   to

uch as o   nswer

eated th   he, "I

you befo   reply.

nted me

ng my ta

es, and o

re, made   l at all

w despis   g

expected   was a

e of swe   lt for

affront a   woman

as by he   f her

tions, he

to be je   friend

eceived s   h. She

ied to p

ed marr   ppe,"

e, as the   you

e your n   s

as to the   it, do

e young

e a subje   n

and imp   ing

propose   f your

nd aunt   ext to

eat-un   only in

— ❦ —

**Their cousin was a
most unpleasant fact of life.
And a clergyman.**

— ❦ —

t lines. As for your Elizabeth's picture, you must not have it taken, for

ainter could do justice to those beautiful eyes?" "It would not be easy,

to catch their expression, but their colour and shape, and the eyelash

CHAPTER 16.

As no objection was made to the young people's engagement with their aunt, and all Mr. Collins's scruples of leaving Mr. and Mrs. Bennet for a single evening during his visit were most steadily resisted, the coach conveyed him and his five cousins at a suitable hour to Meryton; and the girls had the pleasure of hearing, as they entered the drawing-room, that Mr. Wickham had accepted their uncle's invitation, and was then in the house.

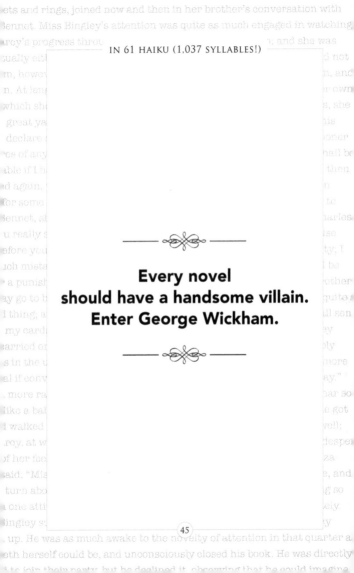

——— ❦ ———

**Every novel
should have a handsome villain.
Enter George Wickham.**

——— ❦ ———

CHAPTER 17.

Elizabeth related to Jane the next day what had passed between Mr. Wickham and herself.

If without disguise." "No," said Darcy, "I have made no such pretension.

aults enough, but they are not, I hope, of understanding. My temper I

ot vouch for. It is, I b   too little for the

nience of   soon

ght, nor   about

very atte

ful. My g   deed!

Elizabeth   ou

chosen yo   me."

e is, I beli   al a

al defect,   your

is to hate   ifully

understa   ey,

of a conve   mind

king Mr.   e

forte was   s not

for it. He   en-

chapter 1

eth wrote   ge

be sent to   d

ated on h

ay, which   f to

e them w   tious,

st not to l   s

t sent the   efore

ay; and it   sister

d them to   ying

, however   pect it

be asked   uiding

elves nec   rage

diately, a   ving

field that   he

unication   aid of

Elizabeth had fallen into Wickham's web. Jane wasn't convinced.

47

g them to stay at least till the following day to work on Jane; and till th

w their going was deferred. Miss Bingley was then sorry that she had

ed the delay, for her jealousy and dislike of one sister much exceeded

CHAPTER 18.

Till Elizabeth entered the drawing-room at Netherfield, and looked in vain for Mr. Wickham among the cluster of red coats there assembled, a doubt of his being present had never occurred to her.

"The person of whom I speak is a gentleman, and a stranger." Mrs.
t's eyes sparkled. "A gentleman and a stranger! It is Mr. Bingley, I am
Well, I am sure I shal   gley. But good
now unly   love,
e bell! I   aid her
id; "it is   ." This
a gener   y
oned by l   nself
ime with
ed this l   t it a
"some de   h, Mr.
, who, w   as he
s." "Oh!   oned.
o not tal   the
that you   ; and I
e, if I ha   or
bout it   an
They ha   which
ennet w   bitterly
 the cru   ters,
ur of a r   most
ous affa   m the
inherit

— ❧ —

**Wickham's absence from
the drawing-room made her think
something wasn't right.**

— ❧ —

s be a li   hat I
e I shall   you at
 very h   ep on
ling with   s seen
e had so   d,
estorha   sisting
n yours   casi-
nd since   wished
 the bre
 lest it

49

with anyone with whom it had always pleased him to be at variance.
 Mrs. Bennet.' My mind, however, is now made up on the subject, for
received ordination at Easter. I have been so fortunate as to be

19

CHAPTER 19.

The next day opened a
new scene at Longbourn.

said Mary, "the letter does not seem defective. The idea of the olive-
a perhaps is not wholly new, yet I think it is well expressed." To Catheri
ydia, neither the lett   re interesting. It

ext to imp   nd it
ow some   of a m
other ec   ay mu
ill-will, a   ure
astonish   to his
and was i   nnet
I said list   ns
d neither   elf. H
tail, heav   ve an
y, and his   before
mpliment   id he
eard muc   shor
truth; an   tune
ed of in i   e of h
s; but M   d mos
y. "You ar   ay pro
else they   You
, perhaps   grievo
to my po   th yo
h things   how
s will go   mada
hardship   it that
tious of   young
that I con   re; bu
os, when   mons
; and the   s of M
s's admir   re
ned and   owing

━━━━━ ⚜ ━━━━━

Mr. Collins made
his move. Elizabeth wished
he had not done so.

━━━━━ ⚜ ━━━━━

his own f   51   uired;
begged to know to which of his fair cousins the excellency of its cookin
wing. But he was set right there by Mrs. Bennet, who assured him with

CHAPTER 20.

Mr. Collins was not left long to the silent contemplation of his successful love; for Mrs. Bennet, having dawdled about in the vestibule to watch for the end of the conference, no sooner saw Elizabeth open the door and with quick step pass her towards the staircase, than she entered the breakfast-room, and congratulated both him and herself in warm terms on the happy prospect of their nearer connection.

, she could not have otherwise failed of, as I am informed by the lady wh
intended her education, and who still resides with them. But she is
tly amiable, and oft̶e̶ ̶ ̶ ̶ ̶ ̶ ̶ ̶ ̶ ̶ ̶ ̶ ̶ ̶ ̶ ̶ ̶ nhis abode in her
phaeton a   her
among ti   pily
nts her b   one (
prived tt   seem
ed with th   ccasic
ar those l   ladie
nore tha   ughter
d born to   f givi
nsequen   hings
. please h   mysel
arly bour   nd it i
y for you   y I as
er these   ent, c
e result d   ng at
ne, and t   rangi
ittle eleg   s, I
s wish to   exped
were fully   d he
ed to him   he th
resolute   tance
eth, requ   he do
een enou   wing-
again, an   the
. Mr Coll   holdi
everythi   ted
and begg   ared a
nd Lydia   olibe
e chose F   and
s he had,   nter-
d him wit   turni

———— ⚜ ————

**Mrs. Bennet was
always one to count chickens
prior to hatching.**

———— ⚜ ————

Richard; and if he does, Colonel Forster will hire him. My aunt told me s
f on Saturday. I shall walk to Meryton to-morrow to hear more about it

CHAPTER 21.

The discussion of Mr. Collins's offer was now nearly at an end, and Elizabeth had only to suffer from the uncomfortable feelings necessarily attending it, and occasionally from some peevish allusions of her mother.

Now, if only her
mother would leave well enough
alone. Not likely.

troduce his friend, Mr. Wickham, who had returned with him the day be
om town, and he was happy to say had accepted a commission in their c
his was exactly   ited only regiment

CHAPTER 22.

The Bennets were engaged to dine with the Lucases and again during the chief of the day was Miss Lucas so kind as to listen to Mr. Collins.

ceived him with her very best politeness, which he returned with as m
ore, apologising for his intrusion, without any previous acquaintance w

s was quite awed by such an excess of good breeding; but her contempl
'one stranger was soon put to an end by exclamations and inquiries abc
ner; of whom, howeve

hat they already

that Mr.   have

nant's co   st ho

id, as he   peare

and Lydia   ckily

ssed win   h with

anger, w   were

ith the P   er

nd call of   ily fr

ourn wou   lips

ted that   ticke

little bit   as ver

ng, and t   is

ies in qui   y that

vers porfe   Jane

he had s   uld

efended   could

re explai   n high

ed Mrs. F   s. He

ted that.   en a

elegant w   civili

en pointe   ithou

y unknow   uted t

nnection   ion in

ole court   young

's engage   ving I

rs. Benne

d, the co   to

on; and t   draw-

om, that   was th

house. W   heir

Collins's defeat
was Charlotte's one-way ticket
out of Hertfordshire.

Mr. Collins was at leisure to look around him and admire, and he was so
struck with the size and furniture of the apartment, that he declared he
almost have supposed himself in the small summer breakfast parlour a

CHAPTER 23.

Elizabeth was sitting with her mother and sisters, reflecting on what she had heard, and doubting whether she was authorized to mention it, when Sir William Lucas himself appeared, sent by his daughter, to announce her engagement to the family.

i talker; but being likewise extremely fond of lottery tickets, she soon
too much interested in the game, too eager in making bets and exclaim-
'ter prizes to have at   ,llowing for the

non dema   o talk
beth, and   ly
ed to hear   ance
Mr. Darcy   sity,
ver, was   mself
quired he   g her
er, asked   ying
. "About   bject
added, "]   stand
" replied
and per a   ble of
g you cer   n
ected wit   zabet
not but I   at suc
sertion, a   of ou
ng yeste   h as
wish to be   n the
house wi   ght to
my opinio   . I am
ualified t   fair
. It is imp   of hin
l in gener   o
gly anyw   ord, I
o more h   xcep
erfield. H   d wi
ide. You   "I
t preten   that
at any ma   him
ve it does
quence, a   s him

When in Hertfordshire,
one can depend on bad news
travelling quickly.

as he chooses to be seen." "I should take him, even on my slight acquain
, to be an ill-tempered man." Wickham only shook his head. "I wonder,"
e, at the next opportunity of speaking, "whether he is likely to be in thi

Volume Two

CHAPTER 24.

Miss Bingley's letter arrived, and put an end to doubt.

Caroline's brittle
note confirmed Jane's fears. Bingley
was completely whipped.

CHAPTER 25.

After a week spent in professions of love and schemes of felicity, Mr. Collins was called from his amiable Charlotte by the arrival of Saturday.

A week of Collins —
and still Charlotte didn't change
her mind. Go figure.

CHAPTER 26.

Mrs. Gardiner's caution to Elizabeth was punctually and kindly given on the first favorable opportunity of speaking to her alone; after honestly telling her what she thought, she thus went on: "You are too sensible a girl, Lizzy, to fall in love merely because you are warned against it; and, therefore, I am not afraid of speaking openly."

t indeed it is distressing. One does not know what to think." "I beg your
; one knows exactly what to think." But Jane could think with certainty

one point, that Mr

**Aunt Gardiner saw
through Mr. Wickham's charm to
his lack of income.**

her surprised to find that he entertained no scruple whatever on that
nd was very far from dreading a rebuke either from the Archbishop, or

CHAPTER 27.

With no greater events than these in the Longbourn family, and otherwise diversified by little beyond the walks to Meryton, sometimes dirty and sometimes cold, did January and February pass away.

——— ❧ ———

January and February. Longbourn. The less said the better.

——— ❧ ———

CHAPTER 28.

Every object in the next day's journey was new and interesting to Elizabeth; and her spirits were in a state of enjoyment; for she had seen her sister looking so well as to banish all fear for her health, and the prospect of her northern tour was a constant source of delight.

————— ❦ —————

**A visit to the
Collinses! A new somewhere
to be unmarried.**

————— ❦ —————

29

CHAPTER 29.

Mr. Collins's triumph, in consequence of this invitation, was complete.

An evening spent
with Lady Catherine was
time forever lost.

CHAPTER 30.

Sir William stayed only a week at Hunsford, but his visit was long enough to convince him of his daughter's being most comfortably settled, and of her possessing such a husband and such a neighbor as were not often met with.

raged from speaking again, and Mr. Darcy's contempt seemed abundan
sing with the length of his second speech, and at the end of it he only
him a slight bow, and

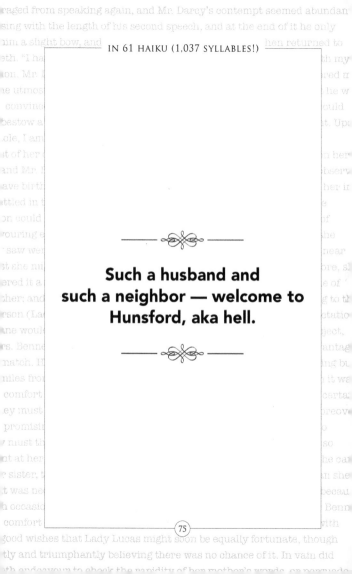

Such a husband and
such a neighbor — welcome to
Hunsford, aka hell.

good wishes that Lady Lucas might soon be equally fortunate, though
tly and triumphantly believing there was no chance of it. In vain did

CHAPTER 31.

Colonel Fitzwilliam's manners were very much admired at the Parsonage, and the ladies all felt that he must add considerably to the pleasures of their engagements at Rosings.

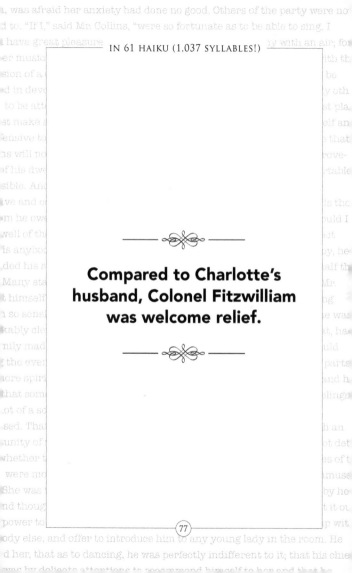

1, was afraid her anxiety had done no good. Others of the party were no
d to. "If I," said Mr. Collins, "were so fortunate as to be able to sing, I

have great pleasure ... ly with an air; for
er music ... th th
sion of a ... be
d in deve ... y oth
to be atte ... st pla
st make s ... elf an
ensive to ... that
ns will no ... rove-
of his dwe ... rtable
sible. And ...
ve and e ... s tho
m he owe ... uld I
well of th ... ct
is anybod ... y, he
ded his s ... alf th
Many sta ... Mr
t himself ... ng
n so sens ... e was
kably cle ... t, ha
nily mad ... uld
the ever ... parts
ore spir ... and h
that som ... elings
ot of a so ...
sed. Tha ... h an
unity of ... t det
whether t ... es of t
were mo ... muse
She was ... by he
nd thoug ... t it o
power to ... p wit

Compared to Charlotte's husband, Colonel Fitzwilliam was welcome relief.

(77)

ody else, and offer to introduce him to any young lady in the room. He
d her, that as to dancing, he was perfectly indifferent to it; that his chie
was by delicate attentions to recommend himself to her and that h

CHAPTER 32.

Elizabeth was sitting by herself the next morning, and writing to Jane while Mrs. Collins and Maria were gone on business into the village, when she was startled by a ring at the door, the certain signal of a visitor.

aration in form. Having resolved to do it without loss of time, as his lea
nce extended only to the following Saturday, and having no feelings of

**Elizabeth had
no idea why Darcy called.
And then just sat there.**

ure, being run away with by his feelings, made Elizabeth so near
g, that she could not use the short pause he allowed in any attempt to

set the example of matrimony in his parish; secondly, that I am convin
at it will add very greatly to my happiness; and thirdly which perhaps
ght to have me   ur advice and reco

CHAPTER 33.

More than once did Elizabeth, in her ramble within the park, unexpectedly meet Mr. Darcy.

all ever pass my lips when we are married." It was absolutely necessar
terrupt him now. "You are too hasty, sir," she cried. "You forget that I ha
ade no answer. Let me do it without further loss of time. Accept my tha

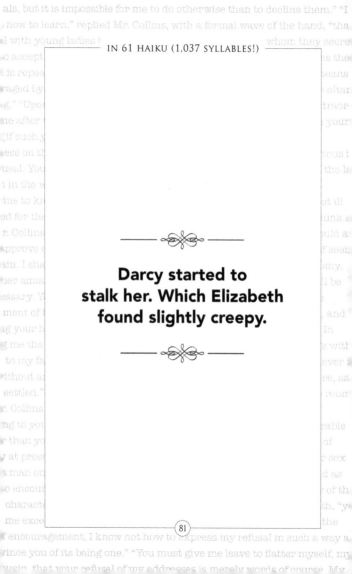

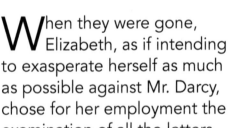

CHAPTER 34.

When they were gone, Elizabeth, as if intending to exasperate herself as much as possible against Mr. Darcy, chose for her employment the examination of all the letters which Jane had written to her since her being in Kent.

t his proposals, but she dared not believe it, and could not help saying s
depend upon it, Mr. Collins," she added, "that Lizzy shall be brought to
a. I will speak to her ⋯ ⋯ ⋯strong, foolish g

es not kn⋯ ⋯n me
upting yo⋯ ⋯ng a
, I know ⋯ ⋯ to a
a my situ⋯ ⋯state.
ore she s⋯ ⋯er not
er into a⋯ ⋯e co
ntribute ⋯ ⋯said
sennet, al⋯ ⋯e. In
hing else⋯ ⋯tly to
nnet, an⋯ ⋯uld no
m time t⋯ ⋯as sh
d the lib⋯ ⋯e all
oan You⋯ ⋯ws sh
t have hi⋯ ⋯and n
er." Mr. ⋯ ⋯fixed
on her fac⋯ ⋯ed by
mmunica⋯ ⋯i he,
she had f⋯ ⋯llins a
Lizzy dec⋯ ⋯s to se
e will not⋯ ⋯ms an
ss busine⋯ ⋯ssist
er marry⋯ ⋯nion.
ennet ra⋯ ⋯ary.
here, ch⋯ ⋯i on a
of import⋯ ⋯r of
age. Is it t⋯ ⋯ffer o
age you h⋯ ⋯e poin
nother in⋯ ⋯Yes, o
ver see h⋯ ⋯th.
this day ⋯ ⋯er wil

**Then he arrived to
declare his love and state why
she was unworthy.**

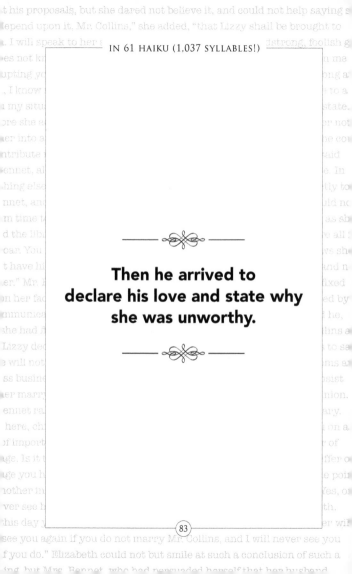

83

see you again if you do not marry Mr. Collins, and I will never see you
f you do." Elizabeth could not but smile at such a conclusion of such a
ing, but Mrs. Bennet, who had persuaded herself that her husband

CHAPTER 35.

Elizabeth awoke the next morning to the same thoughts and meditations which had at length closed her eyes.

s complaints can have no great inclination for talking. Nobody can tell
suffer! But it is always so. Those who do not complain are never pitied."

ighters listened in s   at any attempt to
with he   ked on
ce, with   y Mr.
who ent
ing who   , all of
ld your t   tion
r." Eliza   ved, bt
tced her
d first b   and all
lly were   self wit
g to the
began t   adam,'
he, "let   resen
nued, in   viour c
ughter.   e
r duty o   n early
hent; and   g a
f my pos   r hand
ve often   e
g denied   ou will
ope, con   ar
, by thu   withou
paid you
se your   onable
ig accep   our
t we are   he who
My objec   th due
ration t   been
ehensib   ollins's
ns now r
ortable   ome

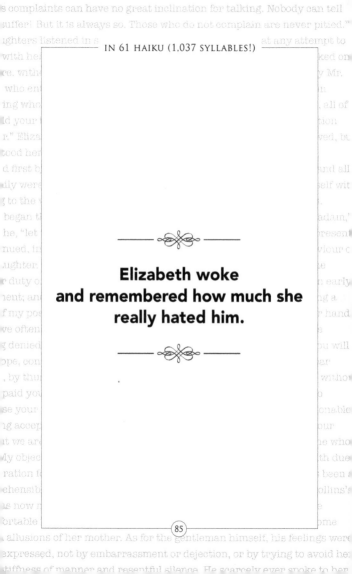

Elizabeth woke
and remembered how much she
really hated him.

allusions of her mother. As for the gentleman himself, his feelings were
expressed, not by embarrassment or dejection, or by trying to avoid her
stiffness of manner and resentful silence. He scarcely ever spoke to her

CHAPTER 36.

If Elizabeth, when Mr. Darcy gave her the letter, did not expect it to contain a renewal of his offers, she had formed no expectation at all of its contents.

pretend to regret anything I shall leave in Hertfordshire, except your
... my dearest friend; but we will hope, at some future period, to enjoy
returns of that delig...

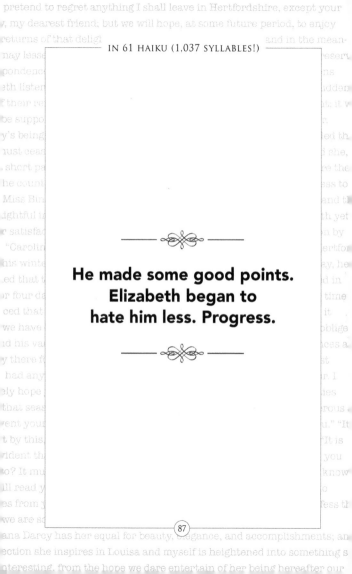

He made some good points.
Elizabeth began to
hate him less. Progress.

...ana Darcy has her equal for beauty, elegance, and accomplishments; an...
...ection she inspires in Louisa and myself is heightened into something s...
...teresting, from the hope we dare entertain of her being hereafter our

CHAPTER 37.

The two gentlemen left Rosings the next morning, and Mr. Collins having been in waiting near the lodges, to make them his parting obeisance, was able to bring home the pleasing intelligence, of their appearing in very good health, and in as tolerable spirits as could be expected, after the melancholy scene so lately gone through at Rosings.

be happy, even supposing the best, in accepting a man whose sisters and s are all wishing him to marry elsewhere?" "You must decide for your- aid Elizabeth; "and i nd that the miser

bliging h being e, I advis " said faintly si ly d at their , and that ch ssion." " be ed. A tho turni e Elizab mere ggestion emen se that th ence man so t ster y as poss re of

its happ

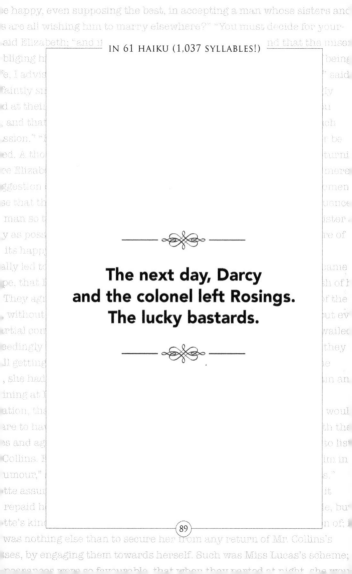

ally led t ame pe, that h h of l

They ag of the , without ut ev rtial con walled eedingly they ll getting , she had an ining at ation, the woul are to hav th the es and ag to list Collins. im in umour," s."

tte assu it repaid h e, bu tte's kind n of;

89

was nothing else than to secure her from any return of Mr. Collins's ses, by engaging them towards herself. Such was Miss Lucas's scheme;

CHAPTER 38.

On Saturday morning Elizabeth and Mr. Collins met for breakfast a few minutes before the others appeared; and he took the opportunity of paying the parting civilities which he deemed indispensably necessary.

Saying good-bye to
a blissful Mr. Collins
took time. And coffee.

shing them health and happiness, not excepting my cousin Elizabeth."

*oper civilities the ladies then withdrew; all of them equally surprised th

editated a quic|

CHAPTER 39.

It was the second week in May, in which the three young ladies set out together from Gracechurch Street for the town of ——, in Hertfordshire; and, as they drew near the appointed inn where Mr. Bennet's carriage was to meet them, they quickly perceived, in token of the coachman's punctuality, both Kitty and Lydia looking out of a dining-room upstairs.

turned to the rest of the family. Charlotte did not stay much longer, and

izabeth was then left to reflect on what she had heard. It was a long tim

fore she became at all reconciled to the idea of so unsuitable a match. T

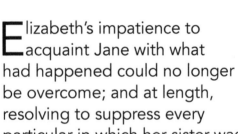

CHAPTER 40.

Elizabeth's impatience to acquaint Jane with what had happened could no longer be overcome; and at length, resolving to suppress every particular in which her sister was concerned, and preparing her to be surprised, she related to her the next morning the chief of the scene between Mr. Darcy and herself.

ger a matter of pleasure to Mrs. Bennet. On the contrary, she was as mu
ed to complain of it as her husband. It was very strange that he should
o Longbourn instead   y inconvenient a
lingly tro   er
was so i   able.
were the g   the
r distres   zabe
omfortal   nging
her tidin   yton
ning no   ly
ed Mrs.   t
alous fals
rent but
ing as sh   , and
orable to   ently
ring. The   ower
end, assis   s of
n might b   t. As
her anxie
eth's, but   twee
f and Eliz   no
elicacy re   e did
k of Bing   e Ja
fess that   sed. I
l all Jane   ranqu
r. Collins   ecep-
Longbou   trodu
e was too   the
, the busi   is
ny. The c   e
mes retu   is
se before   nitia
The very   o an
of ill-humour, and wherever she went she was sure of hearing it talked
ght of Miss Lucas was odious to her. As her successor in that house, she
ed her with jealous abhorrence. Whenever Charlotte came to see them

**A declaration
of love listing all one's faults —
hard to keep from Jane.**

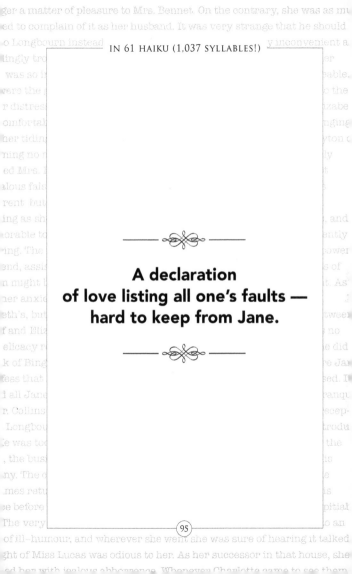

CHAPTER 41.

The first week of their return was soon gone.

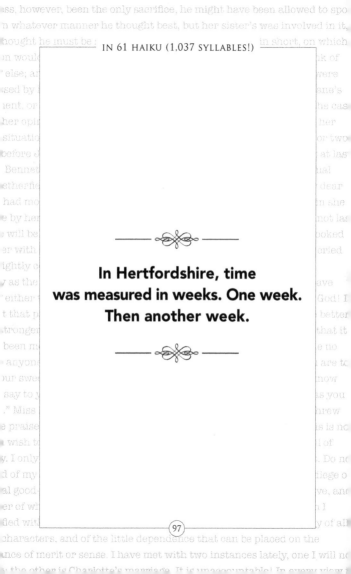

ess, however, been the only sacrifice, he might have been allowed to spo
n whatever manner he thought best, but her sister's was involved in it,
hought he must be

in short, on which

**In Hertfordshire, time
was measured in weeks. One week.
Then another week.**

characters, and of the little dependence that can be placed on the
nce of merit or sense. I have met with two instances lately, one I will nc
the other is Charlotte's marriage. It is unaccountable! In every view

CHAPTER 42.

Had Elizabeth's opinion been all drawn from her own family, she could not have formed a very pleasing opinion of conjugal felicity or domestic comfort.

**Elizabeth saw
her parents' marriage as an
example. Of sorts.**

Volume Three

CHAPTER 43.

Elizabeth, as they drove along, watched for the first appearance of Pemberley Woods with some perturbation; and when at length they turned in at the lodge, her spirits were in a high flutter.

——— ⊰❈⊱ ———

Pemberley produced a flutter effect. Could this be real (-estate) love?

——— ⊰❈⊱ ———

CHAPTER 44.

Elizabeth had settled it that Mr. Darcy would bring his sister to visit her the very day after her reaching Pemberley; and was consequently resolved not to be out of sight of the inn the whole of that morning.

nd in bestowing her tribute of praise on the character of its late possess

s delighting both him and herself. On being made acquainted with the

at Mr Darcy's treatm   some of that

man's rep   h it, a

nfident a   Darcy

ly spoke   tion

eth was p   unity

ng to her   hus

n: "You a   you a

d against   iousl

have you   to

e him in   y

dent. I he   ung

nd if he   not

But as it   ave

and we a

tion and   ther."

ear aunt,   ou to

s likewise   e car

elf, and   n

t it." "Eli   ill try

At prese   ot. B

eyond al   e

es really   ct. I s

prudence   of

e the gr   ather,

er, is par   very

o be the   very

here the   ediat

f fortune   n I

se to be w   , or

n I even   romi

erefore,   yself

—❦—

**She now understood
how much depended upon
his sister's thumbs-up.**

—❦—

t object. When I am in company with him, I will not be wishing. In shor

my best." "Perhaps it will be as well if you discourage his coming here s

ten. At least, you should not remind your mother of inviting him." "As I

CHAPTER 45.

Convinced as Elizabeth now was that Miss Bingley's dislike of her had originated in jealousy, she could not help feeling how unwelcome her appearance at Pemberley must be to her, and was curious to know with how much civility on that lady's side the acquaintance would now be renewed.

**Elizabeth knew
she'd have fun sticking it to
Caroline Bingley.**

CHAPTER 46.

Elizabeth had been a good deal disappointed in not finding a letter from Jane on their first arrival at Lambton; and this disappointment had been renewed on each of the mornings that had now been spent there; but on the third her repining was over, and her sister justified, by the receipt of two letters from her at once, on one of which was marked that it had been missent elsewhere.

——— ❦ ———

The postal system could always be counted on to missend elsewhere.

——— ❦ ———

CHAPTER 47.

"I have been thinking it over
again, Elizabeth," said her
uncle, as they drove from the
town; "and really, upon serious
consideration, I am much more
inclined than I was to judge as
your eldest sister does on the
matter.

It was easier
to hope for the best. Crazy.
But much easier.

48

CHAPTER 48.

The whole party were in hopes of a letter from Mr. Bennet the next morning, but the post came in without bringing a single line from him.

tion of which he attended himself. To work in this garden was one of hi
espectable pleasures; and Elizabeth admired the command of counte-
with which Charlotte ... exercise, and

——— ❦ ———

**In this case, no news
was much better than knowing
just how bad things were.**

——— ❦ ———

our." "Very true, my dear, that is exactly what I say. She is the sort of
a whom one cannot regard with too much deference." The evening was
hiefly in talking over Hertfordshire news, and telling again what had

CHAPTER 49.

Two days after Mr. Bennet's return, as Jane and Elizabeth were walking together in the shrubbery behind the house, they saw the housekeeper coming towards them, and, concluding that she came to call them to their mother, went forward to meet her; but, instead of the expected summons, when they approached her, she said to Miss Bennet, "I beg your pardon, madam, for interrupting you, but I was in hopes you might have got some good news from town, so I took the liberty of coming to ask."

shed for; and that an opportunity of doing it should be given so soon, wa
instance of Lady Catherine's condescension, as he knew not how to
enough. "I confess."   een at all surprise
adyship   g at
. I rathe   ould
. But wi   ld hav
d that v   n,
er, inclu   " "I an
surpris
dge of w   on in
allowed
g are no   day o
orning b   ting
what th
s, and s   hen th
were sep
f uneasy   far fro
g that e   ghter
dvise yc   the
ere is nc   k the
f you fo   f rank
ed." Wh   ir
t doors,   much
l to be k   er
p, and h   d beer
ed to co   sings
much a   . St.
s. As the   a mile
he park   eth sav
be plea   Collir
d the sc   eration
indows
er had   the

"Walking together
in the shrubbery" — code for
"Let's avoid Mama."

the hall, Maria's alarm was every moment increasing, and even Sir
did not look perfectly calm. Elizabeth's courage did not fail her. She ha
othing of Lady Catherine that spoke her awful from any extraordinary

CHAPTER 50.

Mr. Bennet had very often wished before this period of his life that, instead of spending his whole income, he had laid by an annual sum for the better provision of his children, and of his wife, if she survived him.

mminended, first by him and then by Sir William, who was now enough
red to echo whatever his son-in-law said, in a manner which Elizabeth
red Lady Catharine c   emed gratified by
xcessive   hen as
n the tabl   ch
rsation. E   ning. b
s seated   oin w
d in liste   her a
-time M   e Mis
rgh ate,
osed. Mar   en die
g but eat   om,
was little
t any int   ury
t in so de   her
nent cont   ns
rly and   ment

——— ❧ ———

**Bennet often thought
it would be better if his
wife predeceased him.**

——— ❧ ———

ollins, sh   , but
ally to th   o she
red to Mr   d her
nt times,   ounge
erself, w   ey we
ome, whe   t, and
ad been   nence
estions t
ed, "You   r sak
g to Chan
ng estate   r Lew
rgh's fan   hen

ime or other we shall be happy to hear you. Our instrument is a capital
obably superior to   You shall try it some day. Do your sisters play and
"One of them does." "Why did not you all learn? You ought all to have

CHAPTER 51.

Their sister's wedding day arrived; and Jane and Elizabeth felt for her probably more than she felt for herself.

———— ❧ ————

**The definition
of cluelessness should include
Lydia's portrait.**

———— ❧ ————

CHAPTER 52.

Elizabeth had the satisfaction of receiving an answer to her letter as soon as she possibly could.

no one seemed to value but herself, and where she felt beyond the reach

y Catherine's curiosity. In this quiet way, the first fortnight of her visit

ssed away. Easter w   eceding it was to

n additio   t be
ant. Eliz   as
ed there   rnany
usintan   e
atively   amuse
g how i   your to
sin, for   talked
oming w   highe
tion, an   requer
by Miss   rsonag
Collins   openi
nsford   er
his nov   the
telligen   ay his
s. There   **Fifty-two chapters**   r Mr.
had bro   **and finally — a letter**   s uncle
and, to   **not missent elsewhere.**   ned, th
nan acc   d's
rossing   e girls
honou   this
civility   me."
th had s   re the
ch was   hree
en ente   about
not hand   ar. Mr
ooked ju
nents, v   t be h
toward   e.
th mere   illiam
into co   bred

121

nd talked very pleasantly; but his cousin, after having addressed a sligh

ation on the house and garden to Mrs. Collins, sat for some time without

g to anybody. At length, however, his civility was so far awakened as to

CHAPTER 53.

Mr. Wickham was so perfectly satisfied with this conversation that he never again distressed himself, or provoked his dear sister Elizabeth, by introducing the subject of it; and she was pleased to find that she had said enough to keep him quiet.

———— ❧ ————

**She knew that he knew
she knew, and that was enough
to keep him in line.**

———— ❧ ————

CHAPTER 54.

As soon as they were gone, Elizabeth walked out to recover her spirits; or in other words, to dwell without interruption on those subjects that must deaden them more.

she discern any symptom of love; and from the whole of his behaviour t
De Bourgh she derived this comfort for Miss Bingley, that he might have
ust as likely to marry   dy Catherine
ued her r   hany
ctions on   e
rance of   the
ment till
eth was s   thile
ollins an   was
ed by a r   eard
ge, she tr   t app
n was pu   all
tinent qu   prise
arcy, and   too o
g her alor   at he
nderstood   whe
quiries af   total
e. It was   d in t
ence rece   d feel
s to know   re, sl
ed: "How   t, Mr.
I It must   e you
im so so   nd h
s were we   ou."
that she   dded
I have un   rning
field aga   t he
bend very   s, and
ne of life   g." "L
ans to be   urho
e should   a sett
there B   r the
nience of   m to

His behavior made Elizabeth consider hating him again.

or quit it on the same principle." "I should not be surprised," said Darc
were to give it up as soon as any eligible purchase offers." Elizabeth ma

took the hint, and soon began with, "This seems a very comfortable hou[se]
[La]dy Catherine, I believe, did a great deal to it when Mr. Collins first came
[to Hu]nsford." "I bel[ieve] ... [n]ot have bestowed

55

CHAPTER 55.

A few days after this visit, Mr. Bingley called again, and alone.

t returned from her walk. The tête-à-tête surprised them. Mr. Darcy
[rel]ated the mistake which had occasioned his intruding on Miss Bennet, a[nd]

iza, he must be in love with you, or he would never have called us in thi

r way." But when Elizabeth told of his silence; it did not seem very likely

Charlotte's wishes,   onjectures, they

t last on   ng

ng to do,   eld

were ove   illiard

ut gentle   of the

age, or th   ed in it

cousins   lmost

ay. They   rately,

nes toge   s plain

all that   ir

a persu

th was r   il as b

ient adm   and

in comp   in

Fitzwill   rmed

ut why   fficult

tand. It   utes

r without   effect

ty rathe

He seld   at to

him. Co   prove

was ge   ot hav

; and as   f love,

object   ork to

ut. She   ver he

Hunsfo   friend

eal, but   est,

st gaze,   ion in

netimes   wice

ed to El   ibeth

laughed   s the

**It took a few days,
but Bingley came to Longbourn
without his wingman.**

127

from the danger of raising expectations which might only end in

intment; for in her opinion it admitted not of a doubt, that all her

dislike would vanish, if she could suppose him to be in her power.

CHAPTER 56.

One morning, about a week after Bingley's engagement with Jane had been formed, as he and the females of the family were sitting together in the dining-room, their attention was suddenly drawn to the window, by the sound of a carriage; and they perceived a chaise and four driving up the lawn.

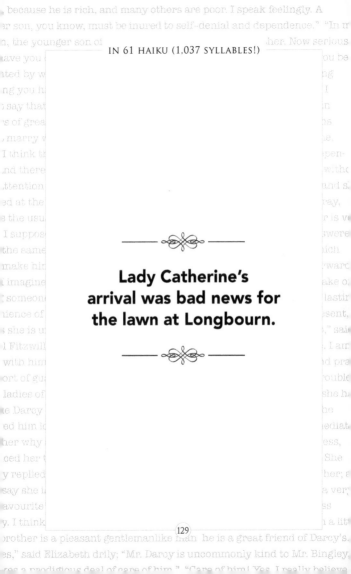

**Lady Catherine's
arrival was bad news for
the lawn at Longbourn.**

CHAPTER 57.

The discomposure of spirits which this extraordinary visit threw Elizabeth into, could not be easily overcome; nor could she, for many hours, learn to think of it less than incessantly.

**Elizabeth went
one-on-one with Lady C.
That felt good. Now what?**

CHAPTER 58.

Instead of receiving any such letter of excuse from his friend, as Elizabeth half expected Mr. Bingley to do, he was able to bring Darcy with him to Longbourn before many days had passed after Lady Catherine's visit.

te of all his endeavours, he had found impossible to conquer; and with pressing his hope that it would now be rewarded by her acceptance of l nd. As he said this, she could easily see that he had no doubt of a favour

urity. Such a circumstance could only exasperate farther, and, when h

the colour rose into her cheeks, and she said: "In such cases as this, it

e, the established m   n for the senti-

avowed,   nat

on shou   you. B

t I have

ed it mos   ne. It

n most   dura-

e feelin   gmen

regard,   nation

cy, who   n her

emed to   His

xion bec   s visib

y feature   d wou

n his lip   as to

th's feel   he said

is is all   ight,

s, wish   n thus

l. But it   she,

ith so ev   o tell

u liked   st you

er? Was   I have

rovocati   t you

y been   k that

siderati   neans

, perhap

nced the   short

listened   : "I ha

eason in   njust

generou   at you

en the p   other

sing on   d the

o its der   misery

**Soon, Darcy himself
came to explain about his
aunt's wacky visit.**

cutest kind." She paused, and saw with no slight indignation that he wa

g with an air which proved him wholly unmoved by any feeling of

CHAPTER 59.

"My dear Lizzy, where can you have been walking to?" was a question which Elizabeth received from Jane as soon as she entered their room, and from all the others when they sat down to table.

ad you behaved in a more gentlemanlike manner." She saw him start at
ut he said nothing, and she continued: "You could not have made the off
r hand in any possibl   e to accept it."

his aston   ssion
d incred   nning
ne first n   our
ars, impr   once
ur selfisl   e
dwork of
vable a di   you
he last n   ry."
ave said   gs, a
ow only t   havir
up so mu   h and
ness." An   hea
e next m   t of h
was now   d from
weaknes   , as s
ed on wh   she
receive   beer
ith her for   her in
f all the   ying
and whic   vas
incredib   rong
on. But h   hat h
ne with i   dging
a he coul
oned Mr.   ed to
soon over   had
ent excit   nd of
Catherine   ter
tte's obse   roke t
orning t   close

**They spent a long time
walking in the shrubbery.
It looked suspicious.**

---

es. She could not yet recover from the surprise of what had happened; i
possible to think of anything else; and, totally indisposed for employ-
she resolved, soon after breakfast, to indulge herself in air and exercis

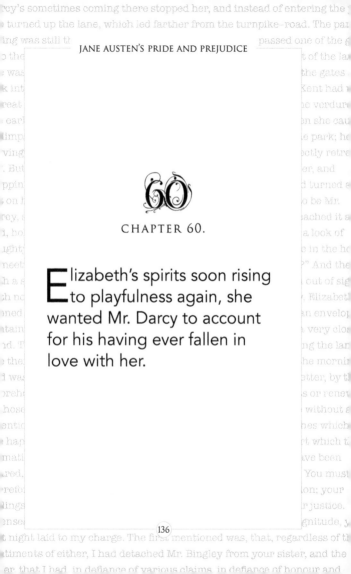

CHAPTER 60.

Elizabeth's spirits soon rising to playfulness again, she wanted Mr. Darcy to account for his having ever fallen in love with her.

am. Wilfully and wantonly to have thrown off the companion of my you

knowledged favourite of my father, a young man who had scarcely any

dependence than on . . . brought up to

IN 61 HAIKU (1,037 SYLLABLES!)

——— ✦ ———

**Elizabeth had
a slight — but sad — tendency
not to let things go.**

——— ✦ ———

the concern which I might have felt in refusing you, had you behaved

gentlemanlike manner." She saw him start at this, but he said nothing

61

CHAPTER 61.

Happy for all her maternal feelings was the day on which Mrs. Bennet got rid of her two most deserving daughters.

e, and she soon passed one of the gates into the ground. After walking three times along that part of the lane, she was tempted, by the pleasan the morning, to stop ... rk. The five weeks

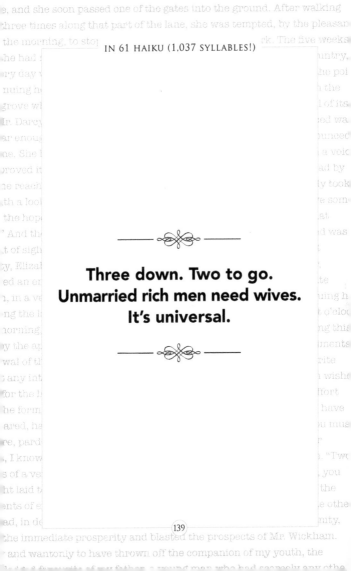

**Three down. Two to go.
Unmarried rich men need wives.
It's universal.**

the immediate prosperity and blasted the prospects of Mr. Wickham.

NOTES

The classic haiku is an image conveyed
with an economy of brushstroke-like words,
counted in syllables (3 lines; 5 syllables /
7 syllables / 5 syllables). Each poem contains
a duality of message (such as joy in the moment
coupled with sadness at its transient nature),
and attempts to answer three questions:

1. **What?** (the object, the action, e.g., falling
    leaf or petal, sound of water)

2. **Where?** (geography, e.g., house, garden,
    mountain)

3. **When?** (seasonal reference, e.g., spring,
    summer, winter, fall)

In this book, I have created a summarizing
haiku of each of the chapters in *Pride and
Prejudice*. This is based on my fascination
with Austen's mastery of the opening line,
which she demonstrates in the first sentence
of each of the novel's 61 chapters.

In so doing, I found that a somewhat ironic and
unexpected voice emerged as each first sentence

became a short poem. I began to hear what might be Austen's acidic feminine wit blending with my 21st-century masculine sensibility — not surprising, given that the novelist and I have been in a relationship for more than 50 years now. And in light of our recent golden anniversary, I can only pray that I have not created a situation in which, as Austen once described some of her in-laws, "a little talent went a long way."

My intention has been to replace the haiku's traditional duality of emotion with an ironic twist conveyed by the narrator, challenging the usual seriousness of literary criticism. But the haiku's three situating questions remain in the background, and I've identified the primary (and motivating) answers to the What / Where / When questions in the following chapter summaries.

NB: These summaries are not meant as complete, detailed accounts of what happened in each chapter. I call out only the events answering the three haiku questions cited above. These serve as background information for the haiku narrator's voice.

Volume One

CHAPTER 1.

It is a truth universally acknowledged, that a single man in possession of a good fortune, must be in want of a wife.

1. What? A wealthy bachelor arrives in the neighborhood

2. Where? Hertfordshire (county), Longbourn (the Bennet residence), Meryton (village)

3. When? Late September Mr. Bingley is scheduled to arrive at Michaelmas (September 29) — *Pride and Prejudice* begins and ends in the fall (hunting season for both game and husbands)

We meet the Bennets, a mismatched mother and father with five (count them, five) unmarried daughters: Jane (22 years old); Elizabeth ("not yet one and twenty"); Mary (somewhere between 18 and 20); Kitty (17); and Lydia (15). The Bennets are country gentry, with no money to speak of, and their estate, Longbourn, is entailed.

If a single man in possession of a good fortune is in want of a wife, a single woman with no fortune at all is dire need of a husband. There is next to no physical description of the characters this chapter introduces — everything about them must be deduced from their conversation. Of which there is much.

CHAPTER 2.

Mr. Bennet was among the earliest of those who waited on Mr. Bingley.

1. What? Mr. Bennet has paid a call on Mr. Bingley at Netherfield Park (the newly leased Bingley residence)

2. Where? Longbourn

3. When? September / October cusp

Mr. Bennet seems to enjoy tormenting his vulgar wife, who is understandably and volubly anxious about their daughters' futures. Mrs. Bennet is relieved that her husband has actually done something to help his daughters meet eligible (i.e., rich) men.

CHAPTER 3.

Not all that Mrs. Bennet, however, with the assistance of her five daughters, could ask on the subject, was sufficient to draw from her husband any satisfactory description of Mr. Bingley.

1. What? Mrs. Bennet cannot learn any interesting details from her husband.

2. Where? Longbourn, the ball at Meryton

3. When? Early October

In Jane Austen's world, parents exist almost exclusively in terms of how much they disappoint their children — and each other. Mrs. Bennet behaves badly at the Meryton ball, and Mr. Bingley's close friend, FitzWilliam Darcy (with an annual income of £10,000), is rude to all concerned. It's difficult to translate the income fueling Darcy's bad behavior into today's money. However, recent studies[1] propose that an income of £10,000 in 1803 would now be worth £796,000 (approx. $1.25 mil).

---

[1] http://www.telegraph.co.uk/culture/books/11063670/Could-Mr-Darcy-afford- a-stately- home-today.html

The two younger Bennet girls have fun with the soldiers (an omen of things to come), and Jane dances with Bingley twice (everyone notices). Darcy insults Elizabeth and puts the central conflict into motion.

CHAPTER 4

When Jane and Elizabeth were alone, the former, who had been cautious in her praise of Mr. Bingley before, expressed to her sister just how very much she admired him.

1. What? A post-mortem on the ball at Meryton

2. Where? The sisters' bedroom at Longbourn

3. When? October

Bingley's origins (and money) are revealed: his family is respectable; he has inherited £100,000 (approx. $12.5 mil); and his parents are conveniently dead. His immediate family consists of his sisters, Mrs. Hurst and Caroline, who seem to go wherever he does. The forgettable Mr. Hurst rounds out the quartet. Jane likes Bingley — Elizabeth is the only one in the family she trusts with this information.

Elizabeth, with good reason, judges
Mr. Darcy as proud. Jane reveals herself
to be a world-class naïf. This conversation
between the sisters is an example of an
interesting facet of all of Austen's work: she
writes about women talking with women and
men and women talking together. But she
never writes about men talking to each other
without the presence of the opposite gender.

CHAPTER 5.

*Within a short walk of Longbourn lived a family
with whom the Bennets were particularly intimate.*

1. What? The Bennets have neighbors
   with whom they are friendly, the Lucases
   (of Lucas Lodge)

2. Where? Lucas Lodge

3. When? October

The Bennets visit the Lucases, who also are
afflicted with unmarried daughters. Sir William
is a merchant who has been recently knighted,
a distinction that "had perhaps been felt too
strongly." Charlotte Lucas is Elizabeth's close

friend. They talk about the ball. Mr. Darcy is a subject of some acerbic remarks on Elizabeth's part.

Charlotte, ever the voice of reason, makes the point that, when looking for a husband, some faults can be overlooked. Elizabeth is not convinced, explaining that she might be able to forgive Darcy's pride if only he hadn't insulted her own. The central conflict becomes more complex.

CHAPTER 6.

The ladies of Longbourn soon waited on those of Netherfield.

1. What? The Bennet sisters meet the Bingley sisters

2. Where? Netherfield

3. When? October

Bingley's sisters soon exchange visits with Jane and Elizabeth. Elizabeth is somewhat suspicious of the sisters' cordiality. Charlotte Lucas warns that women who don't show their affection risk losing out (e.g., Jane), and that happiness in marriage happens only by chance. Elizabeth doesn't agree. Darcy starts to admire Elizabeth, albeit from a distance.

Mr. Bennet's property consisted almost entirely in an estate of two thousand a year, which, unfortunately for his daughters, was entailed, in default of heirs male, on a distant relation; and their mother's fortune, though ample for her situation in life, could but ill supply the deficiency of his.

1. What? The Bennet financial situation is perilous

2. Where? Longbourn, Meryton, Netherfield

3. When? October

Mr. Bennet's annual income (approx. $250,000) covers current expenses, but cannot be passed on to his wife and daughters. Kitty and Lydia are delighted that a military regiment is being stationed in Meryton.

Jane is invited to visit Netherfield, and
Mrs. Bennet decides to send her there on
horseback — despite the inclement weather
and the fact that antibiotics do not yet exist.
Jane gets soaked and becomes seriously ill.
Elizabeth walks through the mud to Netherfield
and decides to stay in order to nurse her sister.
Everything goes according to Mrs. Bennet's
rather surprising Machiavellian scheming.
As long as Jane doesn't die from pneumonia.

CHAPTER 8.
At five o'clock the two ladies retired to dress,
and at half-past six Elizabeth was summoned
to dinner.

1. What? Elizabeth is at close quarters
   with the Bingleys and Darcy

2. Where? Netherfield

3. When? Mid-October

The Bingley sisters reveal their true colors.
Elizabeth and Darcy spar over the definition
of what makes a woman "accomplished."

Much tension exists underneath a surfeit
of witty repartee.

CHAPTER 9.

*Elizabeth passed the chief of the night in her
sister's room, and in the morning had the
pleasure of being able to send a tolerable
answer to the inquiries which she very early
received from Mr. Bingley by a housemaid,
and some time afterwards from the two
elegant ladies who waited on his sisters.*

1. What? Elizabeth continues her observations

2. Where? Netherfield

3. When? Mid-October

Mrs. Bennet and Lydia visit to see how Jane
is doing. Lydia (whose "high animal spirits"
Austen points out) presses Mr. Bingley presses
Mr. Bingley to give a ball at Netherfield.
Bingley agrees, depending on Jane's recovery.
Mrs. Bennet is a predictable embarrassment
to all concerned.

CHAPTER 10.

The day passed much as the day before had done.

1. What? More of the same

2. Where? Netherfield

3. When? Mid-October

Elizabeth and Darcy argue about a wide variety of things. Caroline sharpens her fangs.

CHAPTER 11.

When the ladies removed after dinner, Elizabeth ran up to her sister, and seeing her well guarded from cold, attended her into the drawing-room, where she was welcomed by her two friends with many professions of pleasure; and Elizabeth had never seen them so agreeable as they were during the hour which passed before the gentlemen appeared.

1. What? The visit continues

2. Where? Netherfield

3. When? Mid-October

Jane recovers. Bingley gushes. Caroline schemes. Mr. Hurst falls asleep on the sofa, as is his habit. Elizabeth and Darcy continue to spar, and Darcy points out that her faith in her ability to see things correctly makes her susceptible to her own prejudices and to ignore the truth. Score one for Fitzwilliam.

CHAPTER 12.

In consequence of an agreement between the sisters, Elizabeth wrote the next morning to their mother, to beg that the carriage might be sent for them in the course of the day.

1. What? Elizabeth is desperate to get away from the Bingleys

2. Where? Netherfield, Longbourn

3. When? Mid-October

Mrs. Bennet refuses to send the carriage to bring her daughters home, and the sisters have to borrow Binley's carriage to get home. Everyone is relieved that the visit is over.

CHAPTER 13

"I hope, my dear," said Mr. Bennet to his wife,
*as they were at breakfast the next morning,
"that you have ordered a good dinner to-day,
because I have reason to expect an addition
to our family party."*

1. What? Mr. Collins comes to visit

2. Where? Longbourn

3. When? Early November

Mr. Collins is the heir to Longbourn and
Mr. Bennet's second cousin. A pompous country
vicar, he arrives with a plan to atone for his
eventual inheritance — and the Bennet women's
resulting eviction and impoverishment — by
marrying one of his cousin's daughters.

CHAPTER 14.

*During dinner, Mr. Bennet scarcely spoke at
all; but when the servants were withdrawn, he
thought it time to have some conversation with
his guest, and therefore started a subject in
which he expected him to shine, by observing
that he seemed very fortunate in his patroness.*

1. What? Getting to know Mr. Collins

2. Where? Longbourn

3. When? Early November

After dinner, Mr. Bennet encourages
Mr. Collins to talk about his favorite subject:
his benefactress, Lady Catherine De Bourgh.
The evening ends with a rousing and
vaguely scandalous (for a clergyman) game
of backgammon instead of a reading from
a collection of sermons.

CHAPTER 15.

*Mr. Collins was not a sensible man, and the
deficiency of nature had been but little assisted
by education or society; the greatest part of
his life having been spent under the guidance
of an illiterate and miserly father; and though
he belonged to one of the universities, he
had merely kept the necessary terms, without
forming at it any useful acquaintance.*

1. **What?** Mr. Collins is not a hit with the Bennets

2. **Where?** Longbourn

3. **When?** Early November

The next day, Mr. Collins joins the Bennet sisters in a walk to Meryton. There, everyone's attention is captured by the handsome Mr. Wickham, whose "appearance was greatly in his favor; he had all the best part of beauty, a fine countenance, a good figure and a very pleasing address." Darcy and Bingley appear. There is tension when Wickham and Darcy see each other.

CHAPTER 16.

As no objection was made to the young people's engagement with their aunt, and all Mr. Collins's scruples of leaving Mr. and Mrs. Bennet for a single evening during his visit were most steadily resisted, the coach conveyed him and his five cousins at a suitable hour to Meryton; and the girls had the pleasure of hearing, as they entered the drawing-room, that Mr. Wickham had

*accepted their uncle's invitation, and was
then in the house.*

1. What? Getting out of the house is a
   way of coping with Mr. Collins

2. Where? Meryton

3. When? Mid-November

At dinner the next evening at the Philips's
(Mrs. Bennet's sister and her middle-class
attorney husband), Elizabeth is fascinated
by Wickham. He tells her a story about
Darcy, with whom he grew up, as the son
of the Pemberley steward. He claims that
Darcy's father died and left Wickham money
to pursue a career in the ministry, but Darcy
refused to give Wickham his inheritance.
Elizabeth finds her initial negative impression
of Darcy reinforced by Wickham's story.

CHAPTER 17.

*Elizabeth related to Jane the next day
what had passed between Mr. Wickham
and herself.*

1. What? Elizabeth is developing a friendship with Mr. Wickham

2. Where? Longbourn

3. When? Mid-November

Jane doesn't buy Wickham's story. Bingley issues an invitation to a ball at Netherfield.

CHAPTER 18.

Till Elizabeth entered the drawing-room at Netherfield, and looked in vain for Mr. Wickham among the cluster of red coats there assembled, a doubt of his being present had never occurred to her.

1. What? The Bingley ball

2. Where? Netherfield

3. When? Mid-November

Elizabeth is disappointed that Wickham isn't at the ball and blames Darcy. Caroline tells Elizabeth that Wickham behaved badly to Darcy in some way, but that she does not know the details. Elizabeth is having none of it. Mary displays her considerable lack of musical talent, much to the dismay of the company. Mrs. Bennet is her usual awful self in society.

CHAPTER 19.

The next day opened a new scene at Longbourn.

1. What? Mr. Collins proposes

2. Where? Longbourn

3. When? Mid-November

Mr. Collins proposes to Elizabeth, stating that she should accept him because she's not likely ever to get a better offer. Elizabeth refuses, knowing they would not be a good fit. Plus, she finds him repulsive.

Mr. Collins was not left long to the silent contemplation of his successful love; for Mrs. Bennet, having dawdled about in the vestibule to watch for the end of the conference, no sooner saw Elizabeth open the door and with quick step pass her

*towards the staircase, than she entered
the breakfast-room, and congratulated
both him and herself in warm terms on the
happy prospect of their nearer connection.*

1. What? Elizabeth refuses even to think
    about Mr. Collins's offer

2. Where? Longbourn

3. When? Mid-November

Mrs. Bennet is upset with Elizabeth's decision,
but her father, in his characteristic manner
of thwarting his wife's ambitions for their
daughters, tells her: "Your mother will never
see you again if you do not marry Mr. Collins,
and I will never you see you again if you do."
Mrs. Bennet has a predictable attack of nerves.

CHAPTER 21.
*The discussion of Mr. Collins's offer was now
nearly at an end, and Elizabeth had only
to suffer from the uncomfortable feelings
necessarily attending it, and occasionally from
some peevish allusions of her mother.*

1. What? The subject of marriage with Mr. Collins is closed

2. Where? Longbourn

3. When? Late November (winter is coming)

Mr. Collins moves in on Charlotte Lucas. Wickham meets the senior Bennets. Caroline Bingley writes to say that everyone at Netherfield has suddenly left for London.

CHAPTER 22.

The Bennets were engaged to dine with the Lucases and again during the chief of the day was Miss Lucas so kind as to listen to Mr. Collins.

1. What? Mr. Collins proposes to Charlotte

2. Where? Lucas Lodge

3. When? Late November

Charlotte Lucas accepts Mr. Collins. Her parents are delighted. Elizabeth is mystified and regrets that her friend has "sacrificed every better feeling to worldly advantage."

CHAPTER 23.

Elizabeth was sitting with her mother and sisters, reflecting on what she had heard, and doubting whether she was authorized to mention it, when Sir William Lucas himself appeared, sent by his daughter, to announce her engagement to the family.

1. What? It's official: Mr. Collins and Charlotte Lucas are to wed

2. Where? Longbourn

3. When? Late November

Sir William Lucas arrives to announce Charlotte's engagement officially. Mrs. Bennet is not pleased, to say the least. Jane and Elizabeth notice that Bingley has not written. Jane writes to Caroline.

Volume Two

CHAPTER 24.

Miss Bingley's letter arrived, and put an end to doubt.

1. What? It's over with Jane and Mr. Bingley

2. Where? Longbourn

3. When? December (winter is here)

Caroline writes that Bingley will certainly be gone for an indeterminate period and raves about Darcy's sister, Georgiana. Jane, true to form, refuses to wake up and smell the coffee.

CHAPTER 25.

After a week spent in professions of love and schemes of felicity, Mr. Collins was called from his amiable Charlotte by the arrival of Saturday.

1. What? The Gardiners (Mrs. Bennet's sensible London-based brother and his equally sensible wife) arrive for a visit

2. Where? Longbourn

3. When? Mid-December

Mr. Collins leaves. Mr. and Mrs. Gardiner arrive to celebrate Christmas. Elizabeth brings her aunt up to date on what's been going on with Jane and Bingley.

CHAPTER 26.

Mrs. Gardiner's caution to Elizabeth was punctually and kindly given on the first favorable opportunity of speaking to her alone; after honestly telling her what she thought, she thus went on: "You are too sensible a girl, Lizzy, to fall in love merely because you are warned against it; and, therefore, I am not afraid of speaking openly."

1. What? Mrs. Gardiner proves herself a sensible mother figure for Elizabeth

2. Where? Longbourn

3. When? January

Mrs. Gardiner points out that Wickham has no money and thus could hardly be considered as a possible husband for Elizabeth. Mr. Collins returns to marry Charlotte. Jane travels with the Gardiners to London. She writes to Elizabeth that she wrote to Caroline but received no reply, and then visited Caroline but was coldly received. Now four weeks have passed and Jane has heard nothing from Bingley. When Caroline — finally — paid her a return visit, she was exceedingly chilly.

Wickham's interest shifts from Elizabeth to Miss King, a young woman who recently inherited £10,000 (approx. $1.25 mil). Elizabeth discovers she doesn't much care.

CHAPTER 27.

With no greater events than these in the Longbourn family, and otherwise diversified by little beyond the walks to Meryton, sometimes dirty and sometimes cold, did January and February pass away.

1. What? Winter is boring

2. Where? Longbourn, Meryton, London

3. When? Early March

Sir William Lucas, his youngest daughter, and Elizabeth go to visit Charlotte, stopping along the way in London to check up on Jane, who is

beginning to understand that nice people
can behave badly.

CHAPTER 28.

*Every object in the next day's journey was new
and interesting to Elizabeth; and her spirits were
in a state of enjoyment; for she had seen her
sister looking so well as to banish all fear for
her health, and the prospect of her northern
tour was a constant source of delight.*

1. What? Elizabeth likes being away
   from home

2. Where? On the way to Hunsford Parsonage

3. When? Early March (spring has arrived)

Elizabeth, Sir William Lucas, and his young
daughter, Maria, arrive at the parsonage where
Mr. Collins and Charlotte now live. Charlotte
may not be in love, but she is content. Everyone
is invited to dinner at Rosings, the home of
Darcy's aunt, Lady Catherine De Bourgh.

CHAPTER 29.

Mr. Collins's triumph, in consequence of this invitation, was complete.

1.   What? An evening with Lady Catherine

2.   Where? Rosings

3.   When? March

Dinner with Lady Catherine is not a light-hearted affair. Mr. Collins tells Elizabeth not to worry that her best dress is simple, because Lady Catherine "likes to have the distinction of rank preserved." Enough said.

CHAPTER 30.

Sir William stays only a week at Hunsford Parsonage, but his visit was long enough to convince him of his daughter's being most comfortably settled, and of her possessing such a husband and such a neighbor as were not often met with.

1.   What? Sir William makes his escape

2.   Where? Hunsford Parsonage

3.   When? Late March

As Elizabeth discovers, Charlotte's contentment in marriage is based on leading her life as far apart from Mr. Collins as possible during the day. Darcy and his cousin, Colonel Fitzwillam, arrive to visit their aunt.

CHAPTER 31.
Colonel Fitzwilliam's manners were very much admired at the Parsonage, and the ladies all felt that he must add considerably to the pleasures of their engagements at Rosings.

1. What? Darcy and his cousin make the neighborhood rounds

2. Where? Hunsford Parsonage

3. When? April

Elizabeth and Colonel Fitzwilliam get along. Darcy tries to be friendlier, but Elizabeth is having none of it.

CHAPTER 32.
Elizabeth was sitting by herself the next morning, and writing to Jane while Mrs. Collins and Maria were gone on business into the

village, when she was startled by a ring at the door, the certain signal of a visitor.

1. What? Darcy makes an unexpected call on Elizabeth

2. Where? Hunsford Parsonage

3. When? April

The next morning, Elizabeth is surprised by a visit from Darcy. She is alone in the house, and, in Austen's world, this is a highly unusual situation for two single people of opposite gender. Charlotte tells Elizabeth that the only explanation for Darcy's odd behavior in calling on her is that he must be in love. Elizabeth finds this hard to believe.

CHAPTER 33.
More than once did Elizabeth, in her ramble within the park, unexpectedly meet Mr. Darcy.

1. What? Elizabeth goes for a solitary walk

2. Where? Rosings park

3. When? April

When she goes on walks in the countryside near Rosings, Elizabeth keeps running into Darcy. On another walk, Colonel Fitzwilliam relates a story about how Darcy intervened before one of his friends made an "imprudent marriage." Elizabeth realizes that Fitzwilliam is unknowingly talking about Bingley and Jane. She is furious to realize that Darcy took it upon himself to ruin Jane's chances with Bingley.

CHAPTER 34.

When they were gone, Elizabeth, as if intending to exasperate herself as much as possible against Mr. Darcy, chose for her employment the examination of all the letters which Jane had written to her since her being in Kent.

1. What? Darcy proposes

2. Where? Hunsford Parsonage

3. When? Late April

Charlotte and Mr. Collins go to visit Rosings. Elizabeth stays behind at the parsonage. The doorbell rings. Elizabeth is surprised to find Mr. Darcy, who says he is in love with her and asks her to marry him. He points out that he is asking her despite her family's inferior social status.

Elizabeth, unsurprisingly, is not impressed. She refuses in strong language: "From the very beginning — from the first moment, I may almost say — of my acquaintance with you, your manners, impressing me with the fullest belief of your arrogance, your conceit, and your selfish disdain of the feelings of others, were such as to form the groundwork of disapprobation on which succeeding events have built so immovable a dislike; and I had not known you a month before I felt that you were the last man in the world whom I could ever be prevailed on to marry."

Darcy begs her to accept his best wishes for her future health and happiness and beats a hasty retreat.

CHAPTER 35.

Elizabeth awoke the next morning to the same thoughts and meditations which had at length closed her eyes.

1. What? Elizabeth, once again, goes for a walk

2. Where? Rosings park

3. When? Late April

The next day, Elizabeth takes a walk. She finds Darcy waiting for her. He gives her a letter of explanation about his part in breaking up Jane and Bingley as well as the true story of Wickham's checkered past as a fortune-hunter and his attempt to elope with Georgiana, Darcy's 15-year-old sister who has a dowry of £30,000 (approx. $3.75 mil).

CHAPTER 36.

If Elizabeth, when Mr. Darcy gave her the letter, did not expect it to contain a renewal of his offers, she had formed no expectation at all of its contents.

1. What? Elizabeth learns more about Darcy and Wickham

2. Where? Hunsford Parsonage

3. When? Late April

Elizabeth begins to realize she is not as sterling a judge of character as she had thought.

CHAPTER 37.

The two gentlemen left Rosings the next morning, and Mr. Collins having been in waiting near the lodges, to make them his parting obeisance, was able to bring home the pleasing intelligence, of their appearing in very good health, and in as tolerable spirits as could be expected, after the melancholy scene so lately gone through at Rosings.

1. What? Everyone is getting away from Rosings

2. Where? Rosings, Hunsford Parsonage

3. When? Late April

Lady Catherine gives Elizabeth tips on how to pack.

CHAPTER 38.

On Saturday morning Elizabeth and Mr. Collins met for breakfast a few minutes before the others appeared; and he took the opportunity of paying the parting civilities which he deemed indispensably necessary.

1. What? Elizabeth makes her escape

2. Where? Hunsford Parsonage

3. When? Late April

The next day, Mr. Collins makes an earnest and solemn farewell. Elizabeth arrives in London to visit with the Gardiners before returning to Longbourn with Jane. Elizabeth discovers she is not immune to feeling flattered that someone of Darcy's stature would propose to her.

CHAPTER 39.

It was the second week in May, in which the three young ladies set out together from Gracechurch Street for the town of ——, in Hertfordshire; and, as they drew near the appointed inn where Mr. Bennet's carriage was to meet them, they quickly perceived, in token

of the coachman's punctuality, both Kitty and
Lydia looking out of a dining-room upstairs.

1. What? The Bennet sisters and Catherine
   Lucas head home

2. Where? On the way from London to
   Longbourn

3. When? Mid-May

On their way back to Longbourn, Elizabeth
and Jane are met at an inn by Kitty and Lydia,
who talk constantly about the soldiers and fill
them in on what's happened in Meryton. Lydia
tells them the regiment will soon leave for
Brighton. She hopes to convince their parents
to take everyone there for the summer.

CHAPTER 40.

Elizabeth's impatience to acquaint Jane
with what had happened could no longer
be overcome; and at length, resolving to
suppress every particular in which her sister was
concerned, and preparing her to be surprised,
she related to her the next morning the chief of
the scene between Mr. Darcy and herself.

1. What? Elizabeth tells Jane about Darcy's proposal and Wickham's backstory

2. Where? Longbourn

3. When? Mid-May

Jane and Elizabeth agree not to spread the truth about Wickham. This turns out to be a bad idea.

CHAPTER 41.
The first week of their return was soon gone.

1. What? Lydia arranges to follow the regiment to Brighton

2. Where? Longbourn, Meryton

3. When? Late May

As the regiment prepares to depart Meryton, Lydia receives an invitation from the wife of Colonel Forster to come with the regiment to Brighton. Elizabeth tries to convince her father this is a bad idea, but to no avail. Elizabeth runs into Wickham and lets him know she knows the truth about him.

CHAPTER 42.

Had Elizabeth's opinion been all drawn from her own family, she could not have formed a very pleasing opinion of conjugal felicity or domestic comfort.

1. What? Elizabeth thinks about her parents' marriage

2. Where? Longbourn

3. When? Late June / early July

Elizabeth reflects on her disappointment regarding the example set by her parents' marriage. Elizabeth leaves on her summer holiday with Mr. and Mrs. Gardiner. They tour Derbyshire, which takes them near Pemberley.

Volume Three

CHAPTER 43.

Elizabeth, as they drove along, watched for the first appearance of Pemberley Woods with some perturbation; and when at length they turned in at the lodge, her spirits were in a high flutter.

1. What? Elizabeth and the Gardiners tour Derbyshire

2. Where? Pemberly

3. When? July

At Pemberley, Elizabeth admires the estate's ordered beauty and begins to see Darcy in a new light. Elizabeth and the Gardiners are escorted around the rooms by a housekeeper who praises Mr. Darcy as a kind and generous man: good to his servants, his tenants, and especially his sister. Darcy makes a surprise entrance, but is welcoming.

CHAPTER 44.

Elizabeth had settled it that Mr. Darcy would bring his sister to visit her the very day after her reaching Pemberley; and was consequently resolved not to be out of sight of the inn the whole of that morning.

1. What? Elizabeth meets Georgiana, Darcy's sister

2. Where? The inn at Lambton

3. When? July

The next day, Darcy shows up at the inn with Georgiana and Bingley. Georgiana turns out to be sweet and shy. Bingley asks about Jane. Darcy and Georgiana invite Elizabeth and the Gardiners to Pemberley for dinner with them and the Bingleys the next evening. Elizabeth, seeing Darcy in his element as a responsible lord of the manor, starts to like him a bit.

CHAPTER 45.

Convinced as Elizabeth now was that Miss Bingley's dislike of her had originated in jealousy, she could not help feeling how unwelcome her appearance at Pemberley must be to her, and was curious to know

with how much civility on that lady's side
the acquaintance would now be renewed.

1. What? Elizabeth reencounters the Bingley sisters

2. Where? Pemberley

3. When? July

The next morning, Mr. Gardiner joins Bingley and Darcy to fish. Elizabeth and Mrs. Gardiner pay a visit to Pemberley. Caroline Bingley and Mrs. Hurst do not seem overwhelmed with joy to see Elizabeth.

CHAPTER 46.

Elizabeth had been a good deal disappointed in not finding a letter from Jane on their first arrival at Lambton; and this disappointment had been renewed on each of the mornings that had now been spent there; but on the third her repining was over, and her sister justified, by the receipt of two letters from her at once, on one of which was marked that it had been missent elsewhere.

1. What? Bad news travels fast

2. Where? The inn at Lambton

3. When? July

Elizabeth receives two letters with alarming updates from Jane: Lydia has run off with Wickham to get married in Scotland. The second letter has much worse news: Colonel Forster has learned that Wickham has no plans to marry Lydia, and that the two of them are now in London. The colonel and Mr. Bennet have gone there to search for them.

CHAPTER 47.

"I have been thinking it over again, Elizabeth,"
said her uncle, as they drove from the town;
"and really, upon serious consideration, I am
much more inclined than I was to judge as your
eldest sister does on the matter.

1. What? Discussion of the Lydia / Wickham situation in the carriage

2. Where? Leaving Lambton to return to Longbourn

3. When? July

Elizabeth perks up for a moment. Perhaps Jane and her uncle are right. But she knows better. It's bad. Really bad. The entire Bennet family could be ruined. No one will want to know them, let alone marry any one of the sisters.

CHAPTER 48.

The whole party were in hopes of a letter from Mr. Bennet the next morning, but the post came in without bringing a single line from him.

1. What? More bad news awaits

2. Where? Longbourn

3. When? Late July

It comes out that Wickham accrued serious debts in Meryton as well as gambling debts at Brighton. All attempts to find Wickham and Lydia fail, and Mr. Bennet returns home. He begins to see his failure as father but, as is typical behavior for Austen's ineffective fathers, is only focused on himself.

Two days after Mr. Bennet's return, as Jane and Elizabeth were walking together in the shrubbery behind the house, they saw the housekeeper coming towards them, and, concluding that she came to call them to their mother, went forward to meet her; but, instead of the expected summons, when they approached her, she said to Miss Bennet,
"I beg your pardon, madam, for interrupting you, but I was in hopes you might have got some good news from town, so I took the liberty of coming to ask."

1. What? News of Lydia and Wickham arrives

2. Where? Longbourn

3. When? Early August

A letter arrives from Mr. Gardiner: Lydia and Wickham have been found! They are not yet married, but will be, provided that Mr. Bennet pay Wickham a small amount every year. Mr. Bennet says he strongly suspects that Mr. Gardiner has already paid Wickham much more. He says that Wickham would be a fool

to take less for Lydia. And we all know that
Wickham is a scoundrel, not a fool.

CHAPTER 50.

*Mr. Bennet had very often wished before this
period of his life that, instead of spending his
whole income, he had laid by an annual sum
for the better provision of his children, and
of his wife, if she survived him.*

1. What? Mr. Bennet reflects on his financial life

2. Where? Longbourn

3. When? August

As Mrs. Bennet makes plans for Lydia's
wedding, Elizabeth regrets having told Darcy
about the scandal. She expects him to distance
himself from her now that Wickham will be
joining the Bennet family.

CHAPTER 51.

*Their sister's wedding day arrived; and Jane
and Elizabeth felt for her probably more than
she felt for herself.*

1. What? Lydia and Wickham marry

2. Where? Longbourn

3. When? Mid-August

Lydia and Wickham arrive at Longbourn.
Lydia mocks her older sisters for failing to get
married before she did. Lydia reveals to Elizabeth
that Darcy attended the ceremony. Elizabeth
writes to Mrs. Gardiner for more details.

CHAPTER 52.

*Elizabeth had the satisfaction of receiving
an answer to her letter as soon as she
possibly could.*

1. What? Elizabeth does some detective work

2. Where? Longbourn

3. When? Mid-August

Mrs. Gardiner sends a long reply detailing
how Darcy went to London, tracked down
Wickham and stopped him from abandoning
Lydia and escaping to Europe. Darcy then
negotiated a deal with Wickham and presented

it to Mr. Gardiner. Darcy would pay and
Mr. Gardiner would take all the credit.
Mr. Gardiner resisted, but Darcy argued that
it was his silence about Wickham's character
that created all these problems.

Before Wickham and Lydia depart, Elizabeth
tells her new brother-in-law that she knows
the truth but she is resigned to be his being a
member of the family. She requests that they
not argue about the past.

CHAPTER 53.

*Mr. Wickham was so perfectly satisfied with
this conversation that he never again distressed
himself, or provoked his dear sister Elizabeth,
by introducing the subject of it; and she was
pleased to find that she had said enough to
keep him quiet.*

1. What? Wickham and Elizabeth come
   to terms

2. Where? Longbourn

3. When? Late August

Wickham and Lydia leave. Mrs. Bennet hears rumors that Bingley is returning to Netherfield. Not long after, Bingley and Darcy visit the Bennets. Mrs. Bennet gives a warm welcome to Bingley and cold-shoulders Darcy. She then goes on to speak glowingly about Lydia's marriage to Wickham, much to Elizabeth's mortification.

CHAPTER 54.

As soon as they were gone, Elizabeth walked out to recover her spirits; or in other words, to dwell without interruption on those subjects that must deaden them more.

1. What? Elizabeth goes for a walk

2. Where? Longbourn

3. When? Late August

At the dinner party, Bingley and Jane reconnect. Elizabeth has no idea what's going on with Darcy.

CHAPTER 55.

A few days after this visit, Mr. Bingley called again, and alone.

1. What? Bingley bites the bullet

2. Where? Longbourn

3. When? Early September

Bingley proposes. Jane accepts. No surprise here.

CHAPTER 56.

One morning, about a week after Bingley's engagement with Jane had been formed, as he and the females of the family were sitting together in the dining-room, their attention was suddenly drawn to the window, by the sound of a carriage; and they perceived a chaise and four driving up the lawn.

1. What? Lady Catherine arrives unannounced

2. Where? Longbourn

3. When? Early September

Lady Catherine, in high dudgeon, makes a surprise visit to Longbourn. And her chaise and four drives *up the lawn*! (Austen leaves the resultant damage to the Bennet turf up to the reader's imagination.) Lady Catherine believes that Elizabeth has tricked her nephew into proposing. Elizabeth denies it. Lady Catherine demands that she promise never to accept a proposal from Darcy, as she wants him to marry her sickly daughter, Anne De Bourgh. Elizabeth unconditionally refuses. Lady Catherine drives off (doubtlessly inflicting more damage to the lawn), sending no compliments to Mrs. Bennet.

CHAPTER 57.

The discomposure of spirits which this extraordinary visit threw Elizabeth into, could not be easily overcome; nor could she, for many hours, learn to think of it less than incessantly.

1. What? Elizabeth tries to make sense out of Lady Catherine's visit

2. Where? Longbourn

3. When? Early September

Mr. Bennet shares with her a letter from
Mr. Collins in which he cautions Elizabeth
not to go forward with an engagement to
Darcy against Lady Catherine's wishes.
Mr. Bennet thinks the rumor about Elizabeth
and Darcy is hilarious because he is certain
that Elizabeth hates Darcy and that Darcy is
indifferent to her. As usual, Mr. Bennet's sense
of humor has a sarcastic edge.

CHAPTER 58.

*Instead of receiving any such letter of excuse
from his friend, as Elizabeth half expected
Mr. Bingley to do, he was able to bring Darcy
with him to Longbourn before many days had
passed after Lady Catherine's visit.*

1. What? Bingley and Darcy come calling

2. Where? Longbourn

3. When? Early September

Darcy comes to Longbourn with Bingley. They
all go for a walk, and Elizabeth and Darcy soon
find themselves alone. Elizabeth expresses her
deep gratitude for all that he has done. Darcy

says his feelings for her have not changed since his rejected proposal. Elizabeth confesses that her feelings have significantly changed.

CHAPTER 59.

"My dear Lizzy, where can you have been walking to?" was a question which Elizabeth received from Jane as soon as she entered their room, and from all the others when they sat down to table.

1. What? Jane suspects something

2. Where? Longbourn

3. When? Early September

That night, Elizabeth tells Jane everything. Elizabeth explains how her affections gradually changed, and Jane is predictably delighted. Later, Darcy visits Mr. Bennet in private to ask his consent to marry Elizabeth. Mr. Bennet calls in Elizabeth. He's stunned at the proposal, and wonders why Elizabeth would marry a man she hates. Elizabeth explains everything, and Mr. Bennet gives his blessing.

CHAPTER 60.

Elizabeth's spirits soon rising to playfulness again, she wanted Mr. Darcy to account for his having ever fallen in love with her.

1. What? Elizabeth and Darcy look back over their strange courtship

2. Where? Longbourn

3. When? Mid-September

Elizabeth asks Darcy how he ever fell in love with her. He points to her liveliness of mind, but, like Elizabeth, he can't put his finger on when it happened. Everybody writes everybody else letters containing varying degrees of joy and sincerity.

CHAPTER 61.

Happy for all her maternal feelings was the day on which Mrs. Bennet got rid of her two most deserving daughters.

1. What? Tying up loose ends

2. Where? Longbourn, Pemberley, Derbyshire

3. When? Indeterminate late fall (September / October cusp) and then a year later

A year later, Jane and Bingley move nearer to Elizabeth and Darcy at Pemberley — and further away from Mr. and Mrs. Bennet at Longbourn. Mr. Bennet misses Elizabeth and visits frequently — on his own. Kitty improves in character from spending time with her two older sisters. Mary lives with her parents. Lydia sometimes visits Pemberley, though always without Wickham, whose affection for her seems to have diminished. Georgiana and Elizabeth get along wonderfully. Lady Catherine eventually accepts the marriage and occasionally deigns to visit and tell everyone what to do.

Unlike its opening, *Pride and Prejudice* ends on a somewhat less-than-memorable sentence concerning the Gardiners: "Darcy, as well as Elizabeth, really loved them; and they were both ever sensible of the warmest gratitude, towards the persons who, by bringing her into Derbyshire, had been the means of uniting them."

But nothing could be more fitting that this quiet slipping-away of the narrator and her story. After all, this is a novel about first impressions and only secondarily about lessons learned — as "It is a truth universally acknowledged..." continues to remind us.

Finis.

ABOUT THE AUTHOR

Author of *Everything Becomes a Poem*,
James W. Gaynor is a poet, artist, editor,
and writer. A graduate of Kenyon College,
he lived for years in Paris, where he taught
a course on Emily Dickinson at the University
of Paris, studied the development of the
psychological novel in 17th-century France,
and worked as a translator.

After returning to New York, Gaynor worked as
an editor at Grosset & Dunlap, *Cuisine* magazine,

Scriptwriter News and Forbes Publications. His articles, book reviews, poems and essays have appeared in *The New York Observer*, *OTVmagazine.com*, *Peeking Cat Poetry Magazine*, and *The Gay and Lesbian Review Worldwide*.

As #HaikuJim, Gaynor publishes a daily haiku drawn from current newspaper headlines and is the creator of *Can You Haiku?* — a corporate communications workshop based on using Japanese poetry techniques to improve effective use of today's digital platforms. He recently retired as the Global Verbal Identity Leader for Ernst & Young LLP.

A silver medalist in the 1994 Gay Games (Racewalking), Gaynor's found-object sculpture has been exhibited internationally. He is a member of the Advisory Board of New York's The Creative Center at University Settlement, a nonprofit organization dedicated to bringing the creative arts to people with cancer and chronic illnesses. (thecreativecenter.org)

Gaynor lives in New York City with his canine companion, Emily Dickinson Gaynor, and the cat who oversees their entwined lives, Gerard Manley Hopkins Gaynor.

jameswgaynor.com
#HaikuJim

Three down.
Two to go.
UNMARRIED RICH MEN
NEED WIVES.

It's
univer-
sal.

#HaikuJim

ALSO BY JAMES W. GAYNOR

Everything Becomes a POEM

"With this stunning volume, we find ourselves in the hands of a supremely accomplished poet. The poems are as fine as any I know, and are astonishing for their **virtuosity**, control, and **generosity**."

— **PETER M. STEVENSON**, Journalist and Critic

....

"The beautiful thing about Gaynor's poems is the **surprise** that is waiting around every corner. The first few lines can start a lump forming in your throat, then the last line provokes a **laugh** escaping without warning."

— **ANNIE O'NEIL**, Director and Producer, *Phil's Camino;* Co-producer and Pilgrim, *Walking the Camino: Six Ways to Santiago;* Author, *Everyday Camino with Annie*

"Gaynor's poems are **expansive**, **dark**, **funny**, **full of the joy of living**. His grim acknowledgements of tragic truths are never brooding, while the more seemingly lighthearted verses are deep and honest and real."

— **JOHN S. HALL**, Lyricist / Vocalist, King Missile;
   Author, *Daily Negations*

....

"Reading Gaynor's poetry is like catching up with an old friend, one who's known you a long time and loves you for all your finer points and flaws. He proves himself a wry storyteller, drawing us into narratives at times **absurd** and at times **devastating**, but always leaving us the better for the hearing."

— **DAN CURLEY**, Associate Professor of Classics,
   Skidmore College.

....

Available at all major booksellers, including Amazon, Barnes & Noble, and independent booksellers nationwide!

ISBN 978-0-9978428-0-7 | ISBN 978-0-9978428-1-4

For #HaikuJim workshops, interviews, special sales, or readings, please contact: Susannah Greenberg at *publicity@bookbuzz.com*